222.12
R288

A LIFEGUIDE® BIBLE STUDY

EXODUS

Learning to Trust God

*24 Studies in 2 Parts
for individuals or groups*

James Reapsome

With Notes for Leaders

D0068322

INTERVARSITY PRESS
DOWNERS GROVE, ILLINOIS 60515

© 1989 by James Reapsome

All rights reserved. No part of this book may be reproduced in any form without written permission from InterVarsity Press, P.O. Box 1400, Downers Grove, IL 60515.

InterVarsity Press is the book-publishing division of InterVarsity Christian Fellowship, a student movement active on campus at hundreds of universities, colleges and schools of nursing. For information about local and regional activities, write Public Relations Dept., InterVarsity Christian Fellowship, 6400 Schroeder Rd., P.O. Box 7895, Madison, WI 53707-7895.

Distributed in Canada through InterVarsity Press, 860 Denison St., Unit 3, Markham, Ontario L3R 4H1, Canada.

All Scripture quotations, unless otherwise indicated, are taken from the Holy Bible, New International Version. Copyright © 1973, 1978, International Bible Society. Used by permission of Zondervan Bible Publishers.

Cover photograph: Robert Flesher

ISBN 0-8308-1023-4

Printed in the United States of America

Library of Congress Cataloging-in-Publication Data

Reapsome, James W.
   Exodus: Learning to trust God: 24 studies in 2 parts for
individuals or groups/James Reapsome.
     p.   cm.—(A Lifeguide Bible study)
   ISBN 0-8308-1023-4
   1. Bible. O.T. Exodus—Textbooks. I. Title. II. Series.
BS1245.5.R43 1989
222'.1206—dc20   89-15299
                          CIP

18	17	16	15	14	13	12	11	10	9	8	7	6	5	4	3	2	1
99	98	97	96	95	94	93	92	91	90	89							

Contents

Getting the Most
from LifeGuide® Bible Studies

Many of us long to fill our minds and our lives with Scripture. We desire to be transformed by its message. LifeGuide Bible Studies are designed to be an exciting and challenging way to do just that. They help us to be guided by God's Word in every area of life.

How They Work

LifeGuides have a number of distinctive features. Perhaps the most important is that they are *inductive* rather than *deductive*. In other words, they lead us to *discover* what the Bible says rather than simply *telling* us what it says.

They are also thought provoking. They help us to think about the meaning of the passage so that we can truly understand what the author is saying. The questions require more than one-word answers.

The studies are personal. Questions expose us to the promises, assurances, exhortations and challenges of God's Word. They are designed to allow the Scriptures to renew our minds so that we can be transformed by the Spirit of God. This is the ultimate goal of all Bible study.

The studies are versatile. They are designed for student, neighborhood and church groups. They are also effective for individual study.

How They're Put Together

LifeGuides also have a distinctive format. Each study need take no more than forty-five minutes in a group setting or thirty minutes in personal study—unless you choose to take more time.

The studies can be used within a quarter system in a church and fit well in a semester or trimester system on a college campus. If a guide has more than thirteen studies, it is divided into two or occasionally three parts of approximately twelve studies each.

LifeGuides use a workbook format. Space is provided for writing answers to each question. This is ideal for personal study and allows group members to prepare in advance for the discussion.

The studies also contain leader's notes. They show how to lead a group discussion, provide additional background information on certain questions, give helpful tips on group dynamics and suggest ways to deal with problems which may arise during the discussion. With such helps, someone with little or no experience can lead an effective study.

Suggestions for Individual Study

1. As you begin each study, pray that God will help you to understand and apply the passage to your life.

2. Read and reread the assigned Bible passage to familiarize yourself with what the author is saying. In the case of book studies, you may want to read through the entire book prior to the first study. This will give you a helpful overview of its contents.

3. A good modern translation of the Bible, rather than the King James Version or a paraphrase, will give you the most help. The New International Version, the New American Standard Bible and the Revised Standard Version are all recommended. However, the questions in this guide are based on the New International Version.

4. Write your answers in the space provided in the study guide. This will help you to express your understanding of the passage clearly.

5. It might be good to have a Bible dictionary handy. Use it to look up any unfamiliar words, names or places.

Suggestions for Group Study

1. Come to the study prepared. Follow the suggestions for individual study mentioned above. You will find that careful preparation will greatly enrich your time spent in group discussion.

2. Be willing to participate in the discussion. The leader of your group will not be lecturing. Instead, he or she will be encouraging the members of the group to discuss what they have learned from the passage. The leader will be asking the questions that are found in this guide. Plan to share what God has taught you in your individual study.

3. Stick to the passage being studied. Your answers should be based on the verses which are the focus of the discussion and not on outside authorities such as commentaries or speakers. This guide deliberately avoids jumping

from book to book or passage to passage. Each study focuses on only one passage. Book studies are generally designed to lead you through the book in the order in which it was written. This will help you follow the author's argument.

4. Be sensitive to the other members of the group. Listen attentively when they share what they have learned. You may be surprised by their insights! Link what you say to the comments of others so the group stays on the topic. Also, be affirming whenever you can. This will encourage some of the more hesitant members of the group to participate.

5. Be careful not to dominate the discussion. We are sometimes so eager to share what we have learned that we leave too little opportunity for others to respond. By all means participate! But allow others to also.

6. Expect God to teach you through the passage being discussed and through the other members of the group. Pray that you will have an enjoyable and profitable time together.

7. If you are the discussion leader, you will find additional suggestions and helpful ideas for each study in the leader's notes. These are found at the back of the guide.

Introducing Exodus

When we're young we can hardly wait to get our independence. Responsibility rarely crosses our minds. Our parents, on the other hand, think about responsibility a great deal. They cautiously increase our independence bit by bit, anxiously waiting for signs of growing maturity. But that's just the beginning. For the rest of our lives we walk the tightrope between independence and responsibility.

Long ago this issue was dramatized for us in ancient Israel's struggle to gain its independence and to show responsible obedience to God. Moses was, as it were, the anxious parent deputized by God to lead the nation to independence and to teach them responsible freedom.

The book of Exodus tells it all. Written by Moses himself, Exodus is the story of abject slavery and glorious liberation. Then God patiently teaches what human responsibility means, both in worship and in our relationships with others.

Just like children struggling through adolescence to responsible adulthood, Israel had its good and bad days. Their exodus to freedom did not give them the right to do as they pleased. They had to learn loyalty and obedience to God as a consequence of his giving them their independence. For them, learning to trust and obey God was rooted in God's gracious deliverance from bondage.

In effect, God owned them because he had redeemed them from bondage. The story of Israel's exodus thus becomes a prototype of every Christian's exodus from the enslaving power of sin. Jesus Christ the redeemer becomes Lord of those who would acknowledge his saving love and power.

All this and more is bound up in the book of Exodus. Serious students will find a gold mine of insight and practical values that relate to living today. This is history with a punch. Allow yourself the benefit of careful reflection. Take time to cross 3,500 years and think about both victories and defeats among God's people. Thrill to Moses' encounters with Pharaoh, with his own rebellious people and with God at Mount Sinai. Grasp the significance of the Ten Commandments and the worship of the true and living God. Meditate on new ideas about the meaning of worship, music, and the consecration of one's possessions and talents to the glory of God.

Exodus begins with Moses' account of cruel bondage in Egypt, moves through the bitter struggle with Pharaoh for deliverance, continues on to Mount Sinai and the giving of the Ten Commandments, and climaxes with the building of a place of worship and the establishment of a priesthood. It covers a period of close to one hundred years.

Major themes include the name and glory of God, the covenants (agreements) between God and Israel, the Law and the tabernacle. The institution of the Passover points to salvation through the death of Christ. The tabernacle and the priesthood speak of the God-given principles of how we worship God and the privileges we have to praise and glorify him.

Because there is much historical data to be covered, some of it is not included in the questions. The guide is organized around the major events in the story, their significance for Israel, and what we can learn from them about Christian living. You will need to develop the skill of scanning blocks of text, looking for highlights. Pertinent New Testament doctrines and applications for Christian living are also considered.

The questions are designed to help you discover the facts and to reflect on their significance for your life. The apostle Paul wrote that these ancient accounts were given to teach and warn us (1 Cor 10:11). May God help you to grasp life-changing truth as you grow in your ability to trust and obey him.

Part 1
Liberating God's People
Exodus 1—19

1
Israel's Oppression: Evil Plans, Courageous Resistance

Exodus 1

Oppression is a nasty word, but it grabs the headlines because it's the reason for much conflict today. Scenes out of this chapter fit totalitarian societies. Only the methods of oppression change. God's people were not spared in 1700 B.C., and they are not always spared now. But in this study you will find a bright spot of courageous resistance.

1. To you, what is the most obvious example of oppression in the world today, and why?

2. Read Exodus 1. How did "the sons of Israel" (Jacob's descendants) fare in Egypt (vv. 1-7)?

3. What was their situation under a king who had forgotten Joseph's role (Gen 41) in saving the country (vv. 8-14)?

4. How do oppressors today usually justify their actions?

5. Why did Pharaoh's strategy backfire (v. 12)?

6. The old privileged status of the Hebrews had faded into abject slavery. How would you have felt as a Hebrew youth doing backbreaking labor under a burning sun?

7. What new population control plans did Pharaoh devise (vv. 15-22)?

8. How were his plans thwarted?

9. Imagine the emotions of the king and the midwives when he summoned them (v. 18). What was the secret of the women's self-control and wisdom (vv. 17, 21)?

10. How does your fear of God motivate right moral conduct and give you the courage to withstand the temptation to do evil?

11. The tougher Pharaoh's pressure, the greater Israel's increase (vv. 20-21). How do you account for this?

12. In what circumstances have you felt oppressed by unreasonable demands?

How did you find God's help?

2
The Birth and Escape of Moses: A Mother's Faith, a Son's Brashness

Exodus 2

Working downtown on an engineering maintenance project, the man knew that his friend's wife lay dying in a hospital only four blocks away. But he didn't go to see the woman. Lack of appropriate dress demolished his courage to do something bold in Christ's name. Few of us can brag about how bravely we have responded in crisis. Faith, for us, is a comfortable intellectual exercise, not something that demands bold action. That definition becomes even more attractive when we're not sure how to distinguish between faith and foolishness. This study contrasts a privileged kid's brashness with a woman's courageous faith in action.

1. How has God confronted you recently with a demand for courageous faith?

2. Read Exodus 2. How did God plan for the infant Moses to survive Pharaoh's murderous edict (vv. 1-10)?

3. What did Moses' survival cost his mother?

His sister?

4. Why do you think Pharaoh's daughter defied her father's order?

5. What has been the most costly thing you have had to do for God?

6. Why did Moses flee to Midian (vv. 11-15)? (He was 40 years old at the time.)

7. What motivated him to kill the Egyptian?

To settle a fight between two Hebrews?

8. Who did Moses challenge next, and why (vv. 16-22)?

9. What kind of a person does Moses show himself to be in this chapter?

10. If you had to describe your personality in two or three words, how would you compare it to Moses'?

11. Meanwhile, what was happening to the Israelites in Egypt (v. 23)?

12. How did their condition affect God, and why (vv. 24-25)?

13. God hears the cries of his people today. What difference does that make when you are confronted by circumstances you are powerless to change?

3
The Call of Moses: Stubborn Reluctance Overcome

Exodus 3—4

The milestones of history are marked by people who have met impossible demands. Battlefield monuments utter mute testimony to these events. Modern Turkey owes its existence to Kemal Ataturk, who rallied his troops with the impossible demand that they drive back the enemy from Gallipoli. Your most impossible demand may seem small in comparison—but not at the time the challenge presented itself. Perhaps it was writing an academic paper without adequate time or expertise. Or maybe it was the time when your church group decided to talk to people on the beach about Jesus Christ. This study shows how God put an impossible demand on Moses and propelled him into national leadership.

1. How do you respond when you see a vacuum in leadership in your community and in your church?

2. Read Exodus 3. Imagine that you are Moses on the mountain of God. As you look around you, describe everything you see, hear and feel (vv. 1-6).

3. What motivates God to act on behalf of his people (vv. 7-10)?

What plan does he have in mind?

4. Why do you think God chose an aged desert sheepherder to lead such an auspicious venture?

5. How does Moses respond to God's assignment, and why (vv. 11-13)?

6. When have you felt inadequate to do something God wanted you to do?

7. What reassurance does God give Moses (vv. 12-22)?

8. Read Exodus 4. What other doubts and fears does Moses have (vv. 1, 10)?

9. How does God deal with these inadequacies (vv. 2-9, 11-12)?

10. Why do you think Moses' final objection angers the Lord (vv. 13-17)?

11. What reasons can you give for Moses' stubbornness in the face of God's call?

12. When you are sure God is speaking to you, and a specific "Yes, Lord" is expected of you, what things influence your answer?

13. How do the events in verses 27-31 confirm the Lord's promises to Moses?

14. What have you learned about God in this study that would encourage you to trust him in the face of seemingly impossible demands or difficulties?

4
The Difficulties of Moses and Aaron: Rebuff and Resolution
Exodus 5:1—7:7

T he Christian student group discovered a sure-fire winner for its reach-out meeting. Here was a famous businessman who was sure to attract a crowd. Confidently, the Christians plugged away at inviting their friends, and their work was rewarded with a packed room. An hour or so later they fled the room in defeat. They had tried to obey God but their venture failed. In a word, their hero speaker bombed. Discouragement enveloped the group like a dense fog. No doubt, Moses felt the same way, except the stakes were higher. In this study, he and Aaron are soundly rebuffed, though they doggedly pursue God's will with obedient courage.

1. What various qualities of leadership are required to overcome adversity?

2. Read Exodus 5. What were the major outcomes of the first encounter between Moses and Aaron and Pharaoh?

How did Pharaoh interpret their demand (vv. 8, 17)?

---

3. From his actions, what kind of a person do you think Pharaoh was?

---

4. From a human perspective, why do you think Pharaoh rejected the word of God given through his messengers?

---

5. What things in your life might obscure an authentic word from the Lord?

---

6. Describe Moses' feelings and the logic of his cry to God (vv. 22-23)?

---

7. When your path of obedience to God seems blocked, how do you react? Explain.

---

8. Read Exodus 6:1-27. The statement "I am the LORD" is repeated four times in verses 1-8. What does God emphasize about himself in response to Moses' complaint (vv. 1-5)?

9. What does the Lord's message to Israel emphasize about his plans for them (vv. 6-8)?

10. How does Israel's response to Moses (v. 9) contrast with their initial response (4:31)?

11. Give an example from your life when discouragement blurred the clarity of God's power and promises.

12. Read Exodus 6:28—7:7. Moses is concerned that Pharaoh won't listen to him (6:30). Yet how will Pharaoh's stubbornness help to fulfill God's plans for Egypt (7:3-5)?

13. In spite of defeat and discouragement (5:2; 6:9, 12, 30), Moses "did just as the LORD commanded" (7:6). What do you think brought him to this decisive obedience?

14. What definitive spiritual decisions have you made during your life as a Christian?

Thank God for the people and circumstances he used.

5
The Plagues: God's Power on the Line against Pharaoh
Exodus 7:8—10:29

God's authority is on the line anytime a world leader like Pharaoh decides to take charge. It's also on the line when his children decide to play the game their own way. We have the benefit of looking at a historical book like Exodus to tell us the futility of resisting God. But somehow we find ourselves engaged in a recurring battle in our lives, not too dissimilar to Pharaoh's. Pharaoh opposed God, with devastating consequences. God will also challenge your right to do as you please. This lesson shows that it's futile to resist.

1. In what circumstances have you recently been in a tug-of-war with God?

2. Read Exodus 7:8-25. What was the sign of God's supremacy (vv. 8-13)?

What would this have done for Moses and Aaron?

---

3. What was the condition of Pharaoh's heart (vv. 13-14, 22)?

How would such a spirit be manifested today?

---

4. Read Exodus 8. How did Pharaoh react to these "mighty acts of judgment," as God called them (7:4; 8:8, 25-32)?

---

5. What was the basic issue between God and Pharaoh (7:5, 17; 8:10, 22)?

---

6. What new disclosure does God make to Pharaoh about his power (vv. 22-23)?

---

7. In what matters is God in conflict with earthly powers today?

8. Read Exodus 9. Some of the Egyptians responded positively to this out-break of judgments (v. 20). How do people interpret natural disasters today?

9. What pattern of behavior has by this time become well established in Pharaoh (8:15, 30-32; 9:34-35)?

10. Read Exodus 10. Pharaoh tried to make deals with God (vv. 11, 24). How have you tried to offer God less than full surrender to the totality of his demands?

11. When you are humbled by God, how can you regain your self-confidence and your trust in God?

Think of someone you know who has been humbled by God. How might you lift him or her up to Christ?

6
The Passover: Night of Death and Deliverance
Exodus 11:1—12:28

Death is a powerful, painful lesson. It gets our attention as nothing else does. It's also unavoidable. It was God's final recourse in showing both his supremacy to Pharaoh and his power to liberate his people. When Pharaoh refused God's ultimatum, thousands perished; when Israel heeded his way of deliverance, thousands lived. The final act of judgment is thus a stark portrayal of how every person's fate hinges on either believing or disbelieving the one true and living God in heaven.

1. Why do people avoid facing the issue of possible alternatives after death?

2. Read Exodus 11. What is God's promise and instruction to Moses (vv. 1-2)?

3. How do you account for the Egyptians' change in attitude toward God's people and Moses (v. 3)?

4. What is to be the nature, scope and result of God's final judgment on Egypt (vv. 4-7)?

5. In what sense could Moses' anger either be justifiable or not (v. 8)?

6. From the human standpoint, why do you think Pharaoh was so obstinate that even this impending judgment failed to move him (vv. 9-10)?

7. Like Moses, how can we continue to trust God in the face of seemingly irresistible unbelief among friends, family or relatives?

8. Read Exodus 12:1-28. What steps are the Israelites to take to be spared (vv. 1-13)?

9. Why were they to eat the meal "in haste" (v. 11)?

10. Describe the memorial Feast of Unleavened Bread (vv. 14-20).

How effective do you think it would be as a perpetual commemoration? Why?

11. Imagine yourself as a family head in Israel. How would you explain the meaning of the Lord's Passover to your children (vv. 26-27)?

12. To make deliverance possible, the people had to believe and obey Moses. Why or why wouldn't you have done so? (See Heb 11:28.)

13. The apostle Paul says Christ is our Passover lamb (1 Cor 5:7). What is required of a person for Jesus to be his or her Passover?

14. The shield against the "destroyer" (v. 23) in Egypt was the blood of a perfect lamb. Christ's blood secures the Christian's deliverance from eternal death (Jn 1:29; Heb 9:14; Rev 5:13). As you reflect on the powerful imagery of the Lord's Passover, and also on Christ's sacrifice, what response and deeds would be appropriate?

7
The Exodus: Freedom and Its Cost

Exodus 12:29—13:16

F reedom has a high price. For some political refugees today it means a perilous sea journey along the coast of Southeast Asia. For others, a dangerous trek over Central American mountains. In Europe it often costs job and even family. In this study we find what Israel's freedom cost—both the losers and the winners. God secured the liberation of his people, but this in turn cost them the rights to their most precious possessions.

1. In what ways are we accountable to God for the freedom he gives us?

2. Read Exodus 12:29-51. What contrasts do you observe between Pharaoh's attitude and behavior now and his earlier encounters with Moses and Aaron (vv. 29-32)?

3. How would you describe the emotional intensity of Egyptians (vv. 29-36)?

Why were the Israelites "driven out" of Egypt (v. 39)?

4. God fulfilled his warnings and promises (see Ex 3:20-22; 4:23). What significance would this have for Israel's understanding of God's nature and character?

5. In what ways have you found God's warnings and promises to be true?

6. How would the Passover restrictions (vv. 43-49) encourage foreigners and others to worship God and, at the same time, preserve Israel from religious compromise and contamination?

7. What message is God sending to the Israelites by these rules at the outset of their independence?

8. How can we guard the essential elements of our faith in Jesus Christ and, at the same time, extend his offer of salvation to all people?

9. Read Exodus 13:1-16. God calls Israel to dedicate to him that which he has just delivered—the whole nation, not just the firstborn of man and beast. What plan does God have for perpetuating this ordinance (vv. 8-10, 14-15)?

10. To keep the ritual from becoming sterile, what was required of the worshiper?

11. How do you maintain fresh impressions of your own deliverance from the guilt and enslavement of sin?

12. What was the basis of God's authority to claim the first-born as his own?

13. On what basis does he claim Christians as living sacrifices (see Rom 12:1-2)?

14. In what ways have you responded to his claim on your life?

8
Crossing the Red Sea: From Crisis to Triumph
Exodus 13:17—14:31

Impossible jams converge on us at the most unlikely moments. One minute we're cruising down the freeway at 60 m.p.h., and the next instant we jam on the brakes. For the next two hours we're stuck. Wouldn't it be wonderful if we could wave a magic wand and unclog the whole mess? Life is like that. God leads us in and out of jams to test our mettle. In this study, Israel's moment of glorious freedom was shattered by an advancing army. Seemingly, disaster loomed. But God had some things to prove to Egypt, Israel and Moses. Painful lessons indeed.

1. What recent crisis has brought you to your wit's end, and why?

2. Read Exodus 13:17-22. Why did God not take Israel the shortest route to Palestine?

Of what possible benefit are God's "detours" in our lives?

3. God provided clear guidance for the journey through the pillar of cloud and the pillar of fire (vv. 21-22). How does God guide Christians today?

4. Faith operates both long-range (Joseph) and short-range (following the pillar). What areas of your life require long-range or short-range trust in God?

5. Read Exodus 14:1-14. What plan does God reveal to Moses (vv. 1-4)?

What is God's ultimate purpose (v. 4; see Ex 7:5)?

6. How did the Israelites react to the onslaught of the Egyptians, and why (vv. 10-12)?

7. What did this test reveal about their hearts?

8. In what circumstances have you caved in to fear and second-guessed God?

9. Compare each part of Moses' commands (vv. 13-14) with the Israelites' conditions and attitudes (vv. 10-12).

10. What did God's plan for escape require of Moses and the people (vv. 15-18)?

11. Read Exodus 14:15-31. What was the outcome of this hair-raising experience for the Egyptians, Moses and Israel (vv. 17-18, 30-31)?

12. Think about times when you have felt like Israel, trapped between the Egyptians and the Red Sea. What did you do and why?

13. How can this passage help you in threatening experiences you face in following God, now or in the future?

14. God allowed the Israelites to cross safely on dry ground. Reflect on similar "dry ground" experiences in your life. In what ways have you thanked God for them?

9
The Songs of Moses and Miriam: Praise for the Past and Hope for the Future
Exodus 15:1-21

Music plays a vital role in Christian worship. Sometimes, however, music causes contention: the old favorites versus the new gospel tunes; organs versus guitars. Overlooked is the fact that God gave us music and singing to praise and glorify his name. Nowhere is this seen more clearly than in the thrilling song service that broke out on the eastern shore of the Red Sea. Moses the statesman, Moses the voice of God became Israel's song leader. Praise and honor to God marked the final triumph over Egypt. How much more Christians need to sing to God for his victory in Christ.

1. What part does music play in your worship of God?

2. Read Exodus 15:1-21. What inspired this song of victory (v. 1)?

3. In what terms do Moses and the people express their personal relationship with God and their duty to God (v. 2)?

4. What is the value of reciting God's victories in public singing?

5. On what occasions have you been inspired to break out in song to God?

6. What conclusions about God do the people draw from the Red Sea victory (vv. 3-11)?

7. In what ways do these facts reveal God's purposes for delivering Israel from Egypt?

8. Against what adversaries do you need to see a demonstration of God's power, majesty and holiness?

9. After rehearsing the past, the people look to the future. What enemies lie ahead (vv. 14-15)?

10. What will be the effect of the exodus on these nations (vv. 14-16)?

11. On what basis do the people exude confidence for their future (vv. 13-18)?

12. How does the knowledge of God's character and past faithfulness encourage you in anticipation of the future?

13. Why would it be important for the people to sing about overcoming the enemies yet to be faced?

14. What role did Miriam and the other women play in the victory celebration, and why (vv. 20-21)?

15. In some ways our praise to God should be planned, and in some ways it should be spontaneous. What is the value of both kinds of worship?

•

10
Adversities of the Desert: Thirst, Hunger and Attack—God Overcomes Them All
Exodus 15:22—17:16

One of the premier sports events in America is the Super Bowl, a football game played each January for the championship of the National Football League. Contending teams get two weeks to prepare. Players and coaches get the best of everything in order to win. Suppose the teams ran out of water and food. Suppose the players mutinied. If that happened, suppose you were the coach. Could you possibly concentrate on your game plans? Of course not. But that's what confronted Moses as he led team Israel. This study chronicles not only defection in the ranks, but also attack from outside. Not a pretty picture, really, until we see how God intervened.

1. Describe a time of great team disappointment and why it hurt you.

2. Read Exodus 15:22-27. Put yourself in the shoes of an Israelite three days into the desert with no water. How would you feel and why?

3. God provided water for his people (vv. 25, 27). Why do you think he led them to bitter water first?

4. When you have reached the end of the rope, what do you say to God and to those whom you think are to blame? Why?

5. Read Exodus 16:1-34. Faced with starvation, the Israelites attacked Moses and Aaron (vv. 1-3). In what sense were they groaning against God (vv. 7-8)?

6. What does this reveal about the true nature of complaining about our circumstances?

7. Why and how did God respond to Israel's complaints (vv. 9-15)?

8. In what ways did Israel violate God's commands, and why (vv. 16-30)?

9. Reflect on God's meeting your needs in emergencies. How might you be able to keep such events as a testimony to future generations?

10. Read Exodus 17:1-16. Lack of water creates another crisis. How did Moses sum up the people's failure (v. 7)?

How do you account for their short memory?

11. Israel's next hurdle is an enemy attack (vv. 8-16). What was God's plan for victory over the Amalekites?

What part did Moses, Aaron, Hur and Joshua and the men of Israel play in the victory?

12. As you look around at the unbelief and opposition to God, how might you better organize yourself and your friends to do something about it?

13. Reflect on how Moses summarized the day. What did he do, what did he emphasize, and why (vv. 15-16)?

11
Jethro's Counsel: Enlist Helpers to Carry the Load

Exodus 18

In-laws are the favorite butt of jokes. Rarely are they portrayed in a positive light. But God places us in extended families to give us added wisdom and to shave off our rough edges. Jethro, Moses' father-in-law, brought Moses' wife and sons back to him. He also brought praise and worship to God. But he didn't stop there. This study shows how he made Moses face up to a weak link in his command. Jethro could be accused of meddling, but he was God's deliverer for Moses and Israel, just as much as Joshua and his soldiers were (17:8-16). Jethro forces us to examine our motives in doing Christian service.

1. How do you anticipate family reunions, and why?

2. Read Exodus 18:1-12. What facts do we learn about Jethro and Moses' family (vv. 1-4)?

3. What do the names of Moses' sons recall for him and his family (vv. 3-4)?

4. Of what value is it to have a friend to whom you can tell everything?

Why would Moses have needed such a friend now?

5. Why was worship the appropriate response to Moses' report (vv. 9-12)?

6. In what ways can you draw your family closer to God?

7. Read Exodus 18:13-27. What did Jethro observe about Moses' daily routine and the toll this was taking on Moses and the people (vv. 13-18)?

8. How did Moses respond to Jethro's counsel (vv. 19-26)?

Why might this have been hard for him to do (vv. 15-16)?

---

9. What impressions do you have of Moses' ego at this time in his life?

---

10. Why could it have been easy to overlook God's hand at work in this family reunion, compared to his provision of water, food and victories over the Egyptians and the Amalekites?

---

11. How open are you to seeing God's counsel through your parents, friends, wife or husband and in-laws? Explain.

---

12. Why is it ego-building to be sought after for your counsel and to have authority and responsibility over others (vv. 15-16)?

---

13. For some, what ego needs are being met by their overworking themselves for God?

---

14. If you are in a leadership position, think about planning to share the load. What will this do for you, for others and especially for younger leaders coming along?

12
The Encampment at Mount Sinai: Preparation for God's Laws

Exodus 19

Do you tune in or tune out when the pastor stands to read the Scripture? You've heard it before? Probably. How then can Christians who have heard the Bible so often recapture the expectancy of hearing for the first time? A very practical problem indeed. When God spoke to his people the first time, a thunderstorm erupted. We can't expect that every Sunday, so perhaps we have to look within. How eager are we to hear God speak? To listen and obey? In this study we find not only thunder and lightning but a prepared, excited— even fearful—people. The New Testament reminds us that God is still a consuming fire.

1. In what practical ways can we prepare for Sunday-morning worship?

2. Read Exodus 19:1-9. After three months on the road, what prospect did God hold out for his people (vv. 1-6)?

3. Why would the Israelites be inclined to believe God's promise and obey his commands (vv. 7-8)?

4. What evidence do you have to trust and obey him?

5. Read Exodus 19:10-15. What preparations did the people have to make for God's appearance, and why?

6. What message was God conveying about himself and about his words (vv. 6, 23)?

7. Moses "consecrated" the people so they could meet God (v. 14). What is required of you to meet him? Why?

8. Read Exodus 19:16-25. How and why did the people react to the signs of God's presence on the mountain (vv. 16-19)?

9. Why would the Israelites be tempted to "force their way through to see the Lord" (v. 21)?

10. Moses acts as mediator between God and his people. In what sense is Jesus our mediator now (1 Tim 2:5-6)?

11. What impressions do you have of Moses, of God and of the Israelites in this scene?

12. Why would the events of the three days predispose people to hear and obey God's words?

13. How can we hold God's Word in holy awe?

14. Read Hebrews 12:18-28. In light of Christians' far greater spiritual privileges, what warnings and encouragements does the writer give?

15. How can you be sure not to "refuse him who speaks" (v. 25)?

Part 2
Teaching
God's People
Exodus 20—40

1

The Ten Commandments: Keys to God's Character and Human Welfare

Exodus 20:1-21

The most convincing orders are those issues in simple words: Stop! Go! No misunderstanding them. In military training, soldiers learn split-second obedience to concise commands. Their survival depends on it! In Exodus 20, God speaks ten words—the most majestic moral commands ever spoken, the clearest rules for humanity's welfare. They are the foundation of personal and national life. They also reveal God's character. In this passage Israel learns that God is much more than the God of food, water, military victories and natural calamities.

1. When you were a child, how did your parents teach you to obey simple commands like, "Don't cross the street"?

2. Read Exodus 20:1-11. What right did God have to issue these commands (v. 2)?

3. Put the first command into your own words (v. 3).

Why are God's supremacy and the necessity of absolute loyalty the foundation for the Ten Commandments?

4. What reasons does God give for prohibiting idolatry (v. 4)?

5. What "other gods" or idols compete for your allegiance?

6. Give examples of "misusing" God's name (v. 7).

7. In today's world, how can we observe God's sabbath principle (vv. 8-11)?

8. Read Exodus 20:12-21. How would you interpret the promise given to those who honor their parents (v. 12)?

9. What does "honor" include?

10. Murder and adultery (vv. 13-14) are not just external acts; they are matters of the heart (see Mt 5:21-30). What, then, does it mean to obey these commands?

11. Give examples of stealing, other than burglary and armed robbery (v. 15).

12. In what way is stealing a violation of the sanctity of human relations?

13. What might be some of the consequences of "false testimony" (v. 16)?

14. In what way is coveting (v. 17) not only a wrong against our neighbor but also against God?

15. Reflect on all the commands and, as needed, follow the promise of 1 John 1:9.

2
Laws for Israel: God's Concern for a Well-Ordered Society

Exodus 20:22—23:19

D o not cook a young goat in its mother's milk." That law seems to have about as much relevance as the 55-mph-speed limit. But long before Congress got into the act, God gave laws to his nation that addressed serious social ills that still plague us today. Not goat's milk stew or speed limits—but what about murder, robbery and rape? What about justice and bribery? Who cares for the helpless? In this study Moses conveys God's plan for a newly born nation, whose fundamental credo was "You are to be my holy people" (22:31). Holiness is never outdated.

1. What kinds of laws do people generally like? Dislike? Why?

2. Read Exodus 20:22-26. How would you summarize God's rules for idols and altars?

What reasons does he give for these rules?

---

3. Read Exodus 21:1-11. These laws were intended to improve the conditions of slaves. Why do you think slavery of any kind was permitted?

How does your concern for poor and exploited people express itself today?

---

4. Read Exodus 21:12-36. What crimes are subject to capital punishment, and why (vv. 12-17)?

---

5. What legal principle underlies punishment of those guilty of causing personal injuries (vv. 23-25)?

---

6. How was the welfare of society preserved and promoted by these laws?

---

7. Read Exodus 22:1-15. Restitution had to be made in certain cases. How does being liable for restitution contribute to the protection of property?

8. Read Exodus 22:16-31. In these miscellaneous laws, what do you sense is God's prime concern? Why?

9. What aspects of God's character stand out in this section?

10. How would you explain your social responsibilities based on the principles here?

11. Read Exodus 23:1-9. How does God's concern for justice and mercy stand out here?

12. Of these laws, which do you think are most appropriate to social needs in your community? Why?

13. Read Exodus 23:10-19. Compared to what Israel's religious festivals might cost the average Israelite, what does your worship of God cost you?

3
Ratifying the Covenant: God's Call to His People Confirmed

Exodus 23:20—24:18

P eace treaties and home mortgages are ratified by signatures of the parties involved. Marriages are ratified by vows spoken before witnesses. The point is the same: promises are made and solemnly sealed. God called forth such an agreement at the birth of Israel. A written document was agreed to. Public vows were made. The blood of sacrificial animals sealed the covenant—a landmark in Israel's history. A marriage, as it were, was begun between God and his people. As this study reveals, our commitments to God carry awesome responsibilities.

1. What commitments do you now have that you have agreed to keep?

2. Read Exodus 23:20-33. What perils and temptations lie ahead for the Israelites?

3. In light of these, what commands and promises does God give?

4. On what basis would you think an Israelite could trust God for the unknown?

5. What perils or temptations are you facing?

How does God help you to meet them?

6. Read Exodus 24:1-8. After Israel's response (v. 3) and Moses' steps to ensure that a public record of the laws would be kept (v. 4), why was sacrifice appropriate (v. 5)?

7. How would you summarize the basic points of this agreement (covenant) between God and his people?

8. What is God's basic agreement with you (Heb 8:8-13)?

How was it ratified (Mt 26:28)?

9. What kind of commitment have you made "to do everything the Lord has said"?

10. Read Exodus 24:9-18. What is the purpose of this mountain-top meeting with God?

11. God showed his glory to Israel (vv. 15-18). In what ways have you seen God display his glory in your life?

12. What is the key to your most deeply moving meetings with God?

How does your time with God help you to keep your commitments to him?

4
Instructions for the Tabernacle: God's Blueprint for Worship
Exodus 25–27

Church buildings today appear to be designed primarily for functional purposes. We don't build Gothic cathedrals anymore. We struggle to find God's presence in our sanctuaries. For some, architecture is unimportant. For others, it's a prime source of inspiration. Moses and the Israelites didn't have to debate the matter. God gave them his plan for their sanctuary. Beyond the plans, however, were important spiritual lessons. Fortunately for us, the New Testament gives us the fulfillment of these plans in Christ and his church.

1. In what ways has a particular church building helped or hindered your worship of God?

2. Read Exodus 25:1-9. Why would an Israelite feel prompted to give building materials for the tabernacle (v. 2)?

3. What kinds of offerings does God expect from us (Rom 12:1; 1 Cor 16:1-2; Heb 13:15-16)?

4. What was the purpose of the sanctuary (v. 8)?

Since God does not dwell in a building now (Eph 2:19-22), why should we have church sanctuaries?

5. Read Exodus 25:10-22. The wooden chest called the ark held God's law ("the Testimony"). God promised to meet his people there and teach them his commands (vv. 16, 22). As Christians, how is our access to God and his commands superior to what is described here?

6. Read Exodus 25:23-40. The bread of the Presence (v. 30) symbolized that the fruit of our labors come from and belong to God. Why would Israel need this daily reminder?

In what ways can we acknowledge this today?

7. Read Exodus 26:1-37. What does the value of the materials that went into the tabernacle suggest about the message God was trying to convey to his people?

8. Israel's tabernacle "was only a copy of the true one . . . heaven itself" (Heb 9:24). How does this fact enhance your appreciation of what Jesus has done and is doing for you (Heb 9:1-5, 23-28)?

9. Read Exodus 27:1-8. The altar was the place of sacrifice, which was to be central to Israel's worship. How has Christ fulfilled the purpose of these sacrifices (Heb 9:11-15)?

How do you express appreciation to Jesus for what he has done for you?

10. Read Exodus 27:9-21. Pretend you are standing in the courtyard of the tabernacle. Visualize the scene around you, including the burning lamps. Pick a few simple adjectives to describe what you see.

11. How has this tabernacle plan added to your ability to praise and worship God in relation to his character, majesty and saving deeds?

5
Instituting the Priest-hood: God's Holiness Demonstrated

Exodus 28:1–29:37

Depending on your religious background, priests may be either venerated, despised or just tolerated. Regardless of our church affiliation and the various names we give our leaders, we recognize their role in corporate worship. Too often we see the man or woman in leadership and fail to focus on God himself. The focal point of worship is, after all, God and not the priest or pastor. God's plan for Israel's priesthood pointed to his own holiness and to human sin. Priests and worshipers alike needed atonement for their sins. This study will help you examine your own motives in worship.

1. When you hear the word *priest,* what one-word responses come to mind?

2. Read Exodus 28:1-30. How and why did God give special status to the sons of Aaron?

3. What sets you apart as special to God?

4. What would the precious stones mean to the Israelites in their relationship with God (vv. 9-12, 21, 29)?

5. Jesus is our "continuing memorial before the Lord" (Heb 7:25). What does he mean to your self-image?

6. Read Exodus 28:31-43. What facts about God's nature are emphasized by these garments (vv. 35-36, 38, 43)?

What do they teach about our spiritual condition and its consequences?

7. How can we develop an appreciation of our own sin and God's holiness in our worship?

8. Read Exodus 29:1-37. What offerings were made for the priests (vv. 1-3)?

What was the underlying purpose of the offerings (v. 33)?

9. If you had been one of Aaron's sons, what would have been your major feelings and impressions about God and about your ministry?

10. Why do you think God went to such elaborate measures for his priests' garments and for their ordination?

11. In your life, what would compare to the priestly garments?

12. Jesus is our great high priest. What benefits do we receive from him (Heb 2:14-18; 5:1-3, 7-10; 9:11-15; 10:19-25)?

13. How does your life show your appreciation for these resources in Christ and your desire to use them?

6
Planning the Tabernacle: God's Revelation in People and Things
Exodus 29:38—31:18

Back to the drawing board" is often said after a failed experiment or project. Sometimes Christians behave as though the worship of God is a do-it-yourself project. Some lack a sense of responding to God himself. Church leaders experiment and fiddle with changes in the order of worship. But God is a God of economy and order. No wasted, botched plans or experiments with him. Moses and the Israelites received a specific plan, precise in every detail and dimension. Each part of the plan said something about God. Careful study of the plan pays off in new insights about God and about worship.

1. When you start for church on Sunday morning, what goals for yourself do you have in mind?

2. Read Exodus 29:38-46. How does God summarize the purposes of worship (vv. 42-46)?

3. Under what circumstances do you best meet God, know his fellowship and learn who he is?

4. Read Exodus 30:1-10. Incense speaks of the prayers of God's people (Rev 5:8). Why would Israel need such a reminder?

5. How can you become more faithful in daily prayer?

6. Read Exodus 30:11-16. What aspect of worship would be inspired by paying atonement money?

7. Why do you think it was important that rich and poor gave the same small amount (v. 15)?

8. Read Exodus 30:17-21. When the priests washed, what would they remember about God and about themselves?

9. The Bible speaks of the cleansing effect of Scripture (Ps 119:9; Jn 15:3). Why is it important to be washed daily by God's Word?

10. Read Exodus 30:22-38. The sacred anointing oil signified holiness (v. 29). In what ways are Christians set apart for holy uses by God?

11. Read Exodus 31:1-11. The shepherds of Israel had neither artistic skills nor craftsmanship. What does God's plan to remedy this reveal about his concern for beauty?

12. What has God uniquely gifted you to do?

13. Read Exodus 31:12-18. This is the third instruction and warning regarding the Sabbath (see 20:8-11; 23:10-13). What new emphasis is added here regarding the purpose of the Sabbath and the punishment of those who disregard it?

14. From these forty days' instructions (Ex 25—31) by God, what major impressions do you receive about him and about worshiping him?

How do these impressions affect your own worship?

7
The Golden Calf: Idolatry Takes a Fearful Toll

Exodus 32

P robably nothing shocks us as much as defection. Selling out to the enemy is hard to understand. Loyalty rightly stands near the top of qualities we admire. When traitors are exposed, we smugly assume that we would never do such a thing. But who knows where we are the most vulnerable? On the heels of glorious triumph, Israel plunged into idolatry on the flimsiest of excuses. God's nation flunked the loyalty test, with disastrous consequences.

1. It's been said that every person has a price. In what areas might you be most susceptible to betraying God, and why?

2. Read Exodus 32:1-6. Who instigated the idolatry, and why (v. 1)?

3. Why do you think Aaron went along with it (vv. 2-6)?

4. Read Exodus 32:7-14. What impresses you about the dialog between God and Moses (vv. 9-14)?

5. In what ways can we emulate Moses in our relation to God and in our care for sinning people?

6. Read Exodus 32:15-24. How did Moses react when he saw the Israelites' idolatrous worship (vv. 19-24)?

7. Why do you think Aaron lied to Moses (vv. 22-24)?

8. What positive and negative examples of spiritual leadership do you see here?

9. In what situations have you exercised, or failed to exercise, a strong stand against clear-cut violations of God's commands? Explain.

10. Read Exodus 32:25-35. How was God's judgment against idolatry carried out (vv. 27-28, 35)?

11. What did it cost the Levites to take a public stand for God?

12. Moses offered his life to atone for Israel's sin (vv. 30-32). What did God promise instead (vv. 33-34)?

13. What character qualities does Moses demonstrate in this incident?

How do you account for them?

14. What spiritual disciplines could help you maintain faithfulness to God?

8
God's Presence and Glory: Essential Requirement and Goal
Exodus 33

I remember taking my son to school the first time. I dragged him all the way. My presence was not enough to enable him to face this terrible prospect. The command to go was clear, but that wasn't enough for him. God commanded Israel to go to the good land he had promised to give them. God's leader asked for God's presence before he would move out. In this study we see more of God's loving patience with Moses and Israel, and how this speaks to our own basic spiritual goals.

1. In what circumstances have you felt a special need of God's presence, and why?

2. Read Exodus 33:1-6. What commands, promises and warning did God give Israel?

3. What does it mean to be a "stiff-necked people" (vv. 3, 5)?

How would such a person be described today?

4. What can we do to avoid this condition?

5. Read Exodus 33:7-11. What occurred at the tent of meeting, and why?

6. What do these verses reveal about Moses' relationship with God and the effect it had on others?

7. What would it take for you to develop such a relationship?

What would it do for you and for God?

8. Read Exodus 33:12-23. Look at the development of Moses' requests (vv. 13, 15, 18). How do they increase in spiritual wisdom and depth and reveal Moses' deepest desire?

9. God allowed Moses to hear his name proclaimed (v. 19). What did this add to their relationship?

10. In God's answer to Moses (vv. 19-23), what do you learn about his nature and character?

11. How has the Lord demonstrated these qualities in Exodus?

12. Moses could not see God's face. What is our privilege and responsibility in light of John 14:8-14 and Hebrews 1:1-4?

13. In what ways do you demonstrate a desire to know God and to see his glory?

How has God honored your requests?

9
Renewing the Covenant: God Reveals His Nature and Laws—Again
Exodus 34

T he cynical statement of some historians is that treaties are made to be broken. Sadly, that's often been the case. Man's record of keeping treaties is abysmal, but nations keep on making treaties, hoping for a more secure future. Israel fell into idolatry and soon broke faith with God (Ex 19:8; 24:3). Likewise, we can recall solemn vows and promises shattered by expediency, fear and unfaithfulness. But God doesn't quit on us. That's not his nature. In this study, he calls Moses to the mountain a second time and reaffirms principles of holy living.

1. Think of an experience in which you were given a second chance. How did it make you feel? Why?

2. Read Exodus 34:1-9. In order to meet God, what was required of Moses, and why (vv. 1-3)?

3. How would you describe God, based on what he proclaimed to Moses (vv. 6-7)?

Why did Moses need this reminder?

4. How can you develop an appreciation for each aspect of God's nature?

5. What request did Moses make, and why (vv. 8-9)?

6. Read Exodus 34:10-28. How would you summarize the covenant God made with Israel?

7. Of all the laws previously given, why do you think these are emphasized at this time?

8. God calls us to live among those who do not honor his name. In what ways can they be a "snare" for us (v. 12)?

9. What principles of godly living in the New Testament would correspond to God's concern for Israel here (Gal 5:16-26; Eph 4:20-32)?

10. Read Exodus 34:29-35. What effect did this meeting with God have on Moses, the leaders and the people (vv. 29-32)?

11. What practice was then established, and why (vv. 33-35)?

12. What greater privilege is ours in Christ (2 Cor 3:18)?

13. What is required of us if we are to reflect God's glory?

14. God gave Israel a second chance, so to speak. What is there in this experience to encourage you to keep on in faith and obedience to God?

10
Building the Tabernacle: More Than Enough to Do the Job
Exodus 35—36

Hardly a day passes that we aren't asked to contribute to some worthy cause, or implored to work on a needed project. The avalanche of appeals dulls our senses and makes it hard to sort out priorities. It's tempting to do nothing. In this study, God launches a tabernacle building project. He asks for money (donated goods) and services (labor). Israel was called a "stiffed-necked people"—not the best prospects for a building fund drive—but their response to God is surprising.

1. To what needs are you giving time or money, and why?

2. Read Exodus 35:1-29. What was God's plan for the provision of materials (vv. 4-9)?

3. What factors would an Israelite weigh in deciding whether or not to give?

4. Of what value and importance would it be for the Israelites to give their own possessions and to build the tabernacle themselves (v. 10)?

5. The Israelites responded to God's call for an offering (vv. 20-29). How do you account for this outpouring of goods and materials (see 36:3-7)?

6. In God's plan, how was it possible for everyone to give something (see 3:21-22; 12:35-36)?

7. Read Exodus 35:30—36:7. How did the nomadic Israelites—shepherds in Egypt for more than four centuries—suddenly develop skills in design, building and craftsmanship (vv. 30-35)?

8. Who came to do the work (36:1-2)?

What problem did they encounter (vv. 3-7)?

9. Read Exodus 36:8-38. What impressions of the design and beauty of the tabernacle do you gain from this description?

10. What possessions and abilities do you have for God to use?

What has he shown you about how to use them for his service?

11. What keeps God's people today from giving willingly, sacrificially and generously?

12. What would it take in your church to produce an outpouring of goods and services for God's use, like that of the Israelites (see 2 Cor 8:1-5)?

11
Making Furnishings and Garments: God Speaks Powerfully in Wood, Gold, Silver, Linen and Wool
Exodus 37:1—39:31

H̲ow important is the furniture in your church? What about the clothes people wear? What do they say to you and others? In God's plan for Israel's worship, he spoke powerfully through furniture and clothing. God has also given us spiritual dress—both inner qualities and outward deeds—to help people know and understand him. He also speaks to us in the beauty of the sanctuary. This study looks at outward things, so look for their hidden meaning and significance. The medium is the message in this case.

---

1. How could a cabinetmaker and a seamstress glorify God in their work?

---

2. Read Exodus 37—38. How would the ark, table, lampstand, altar of incense and altar of burnt offering assist the Israelites in their worship of God?

3. What aspect of God's nature and character does each article depict?

4. How does each article illustrate some aspect of our own relation to God?

5. What advantages do we have in knowing and worshiping God that the Israelites did not have (Heb 9:1-15)?

6. Read Exodus 39. What message was God trying to convey about himself and worship through the ephod, breastpiece, robe and tunic of the priests?

7. The New Testament refers to Christians as priests (1 Pet 2:5, 9). What is our function as priests?

8. What priestly garments are we called to wear (Col 3:12-14)?

9. How would these qualities help us in our role as priests?

---

10. Fine linen (Ex 38:9; 39:3, 5, 8, 27) appears again at the consummation of God's plan for his people. It will be the clothing of Christ's bride, the church. What does it represent (Rev 19:8)?

As one of God's saints, what does the significance of fine linen inspire you to do and to anticipate?

12
Dedicating the Tabernacle: Time for Praise and Reflection
Exodus 39:32—40:38

Dedications of new churches are special. Such services evoke pride and appreciation. But with every privilege and blessing from God comes new responsibilities. Our church buildings, in a sense, call us to faithful worship, witness and obedience to God's will. Although God's glory may not be visible, it is present in our hearts. Join with Moses and the Israelites in this study and celebrate God's goodness to them and to us.

1. In what circumstances have you especially felt God's presence, and why?

2. Read Exodus 39:32-43. What feelings do you think the Israelites had in working "just as the Lord had commanded" and in showing their work to Moses?

3. As you invest your life for God, what satisfaction have you gained from following his blueprint?

4. Read Exodus 40:1-33. Why was it necessary to anoint everything, to burn incense and make offerings (vv. 9-10, 26-29)?

5. Buildings and furnishings today are not holy, as the tabernacle and its furnishings were. What are the components of God's dwelling place today (Eph 2:19-22)?

6. What care are we to take in constructing God's dwelling place, and why (1 Cor 3:9-17)?

7. Read Exodus 40:34-38. How did God reveal his presence?

8. What do you think "the glory of the Lord" resembled?

9. How does God reveal his glory and presence in our midst today?

10. Imagine the feelings of the Israelites on this day. What reasons would they have had for these feelings?

11. Thirteen chapters of Exodus deal with the tabernacle and the priesthood. What important lessons did God intend for his people to learn through them?

12. What major lessons has God taught you about your life with him through studying Exodus?

Leader's Notes

Leading a Bible discussion can be an enjoyable and rewarding experience. But it can also be *scary*—especially if you've never done it before. If this is your feeling, you're in good company. When God asked Moses to lead the Israelites out of Egypt, he replied, "O Lord, please send someone else to do it!" (Ex 4:13).

When Solomon became king of Israel, he felt the task was far beyond his abilities. "I am only a little child and do not know how to carry out my duties. . . . Who is able to govern this great people of yours?" (1 Kings 3:7, 9).

When God called Jeremiah to be a prophet, he replied, "Ah, Sovereign LORD, . . . I do not know how to speak; I am only a child" (Jer 1:6).

The list goes on. The apostles were "unschooled, ordinary men" (Acts 4:13). Timothy was young, frail and frightened. Paul's "thorn in the flesh" made him feel weak. But God's response to all of his servants—including you—is essentially the same: "My grace is sufficient for you" (2 Cor 12:9). Relax. God helped these people in spite of their weaknesses, and he can help you in spite of your feelings of inadequacy.

There is another reason why you should feel encouraged. Leading a Bible discussion is not difficult if you follow certain guidelines. You don't need to be an expert on the Bible or a trained teacher. The suggestions listed below should enable you to effectively and enjoyably fulfill your role as leader.

Preparing to Lead

1. Ask God to help you understand and apply the passage to your own life. Unless this happens, you will not be prepared to lead others. Pray too for the various members of the group. Ask God to give you an enjoyable and profitable time together studying his Word.

2. As you begin each study, read and reread the assigned Bible passage to familiarize yourself with what the author is saying. In the case of book studies, you may want to read through the entire book prior to the first study. This will give you a helpful overview of its contents.

3. This study guide is based on the New International Version of the Bible. It will help you and the group if you use this translation as the basis for your study and discussion. Encourage others to use the NIV also, but allow them the freedom to use whatever translation they prefer.

4. Carefully work through each question in the study. Spend time in meditation and reflection as you formulate your answers.

5. Write your answers in the space provided in the study guide. This will help you to express your understanding of the passage clearly.

6. It might help you to have a Bible dictionary handy. Use it to look up any unfamiliar words, names or places. (For additional help on how to study a passage, see chapter five of *Leading Bible Discussions,* IVP.)

7. Once you have finished your own study of the passage, familiarize yourself with the leader's notes for the study you are leading. These are designed to help you in several ways. First, they tell you the purpose the study guide author had in mind while writing the study. Take time to think through how the study questions work together to accomplish that purpose. Second, the notes provide you with additional background information or comments on some of the questions. This information can be useful if people have difficulty understanding or answering a question. Third, the leader's notes can alert you to potential problems you may encounter during the study.

8. If you wish to remind yourself of anything mentioned in the leader's notes, make a note to yourself below that question in the study.

Leading the Study

1. Begin the study on time. Unless you are leading an evangelistic Bible study, open with prayer, asking God to help you to understand and apply the passage.

2. Be sure that everyone in your group has a study guide. Encourage them to prepare beforehand for each discussion by working through the questions in the guide.

3. At the beginning of your first time together, explain that these studies are meant to be discussions not lectures. Encourage the members of the group to participate. However, do not put pressure on those who may be hesitant to speak during the first few sessions.

4. Read the introductory paragraph at the beginning of the discussion. This will orient the group to the passage being studied.

5. Read the passage aloud if you are studying one chapter or less. You may choose to do this yourself, or someone else may read if he or she has been asked to do so prior to the study. Longer passages may occasionally be read in parts at different times during the study. Some studies may cover several chapters. In such cases reading aloud would probably take too much time, so the group members should simply read the assigned passages prior to the study.

6. As you begin to ask the questions in the guide, keep several things in mind. First, the questions are designed to be used just as they are written. If you wish, you may simply read them aloud to the group. Or you may prefer to express them in your own words. However, unnecessary rewording of the questions is not recommended.

Second, the questions are intended to guide the group toward understanding and applying the *main idea* of the passage. The author of the guide has stated his or her view of this central idea in the *purpose* of the study in the leader's notes. You should try to understand how the passage expresses this idea and how the study questions work together to lead the group in that direction.

There may be times when it is appropriate to deviate from the study guide. For example, a question may have already been answered. If so, move on to the next question. Or someone may raise an important question not covered in the guide. Take time to discuss it! The important thing is to use discretion. There may be many routes you can travel to reach the goal of the study. But the easiest route is usually the one the author has suggested.

7. Avoid answering your own questions. If necessary, repeat or rephrase them until they are clearly understood. An eager group quickly becomes passive and silent if they think the leader will do most of the talking.

8. Don't be afraid of silence. People may need time to think about the question before formulating their answers.

9. Don't be content with just one answer. Ask, "What do the rest of you think?" or "Anything else?" until several people have given answers to the question.

10. Acknowledge all contributions. Try to be affirming whenever possible. Never reject an answer. If it is clearly wrong, ask, "Which verse led you to that conclusion?" or again, "What do the rest of you think?"

11. Don't expect every answer to be addressed to you, even though this will probably happen at first. As group members become more at ease, they will begin to truly interact with each other. This is one sign of a healthy discussion.

12. Don't be afraid of controversy. It can be very stimulating. If you don't resolve an issue completely, don't be frustrated. Move on and keep it in mind for later. A subsequent study may solve the problem.

13. Stick to the passage under consideration. It should be the source for answering the questions. Discourage the group from unnecessary cross-referencing. Likewise, stick to the subject and avoid going off on tangents.

14. Periodically summarize what the *group* has said about the passage. This helps to draw together the various ideas mentioned and gives continuity to the study. But don't preach.

15. Conclude your time together with conversational prayer. Be sure to ask God's help to apply those things which you learned in the study.

16. End on time.

Many more suggestions and helps are found in *Leading Bible Discussions* (IVP). Reading and studying through that would be well worth your time.

Components of Small Groups

A healthy small group should do more than study the Bible. There are four components you should consider as you structure your time together.

Nurture. Being a part of a small group should be a nurturing and edifying experience. You should grow in your knowledge and love of God and each other. If we are to properly love God, we must know and keep his commandments (Jn 14:15). That is why Bible study should be a foundational part of your small group. But you can be nurtured by other things as well. You can memorize Scripture, read and discuss a book, or occasionally listen to a tape of a good speaker.

Community. Most people have a need for close friendships. Your small group can be an excellent place to cultivate such relationships. Allow time for informal interaction before and after the study. Have a time of sharing during the meeting. Do fun things together as a group, such as a potluck supper or a picnic. Have someone bring refreshments to the meeting. Be creative!

Worship. A portion of your time together can be spent in worship and prayer. Praise God together for who he is. Thank him for what he has done and is doing in your lives and in the world. Pray for each other's needs. Ask God to help you to apply what you have learned. Sing hymns together.

Mission. Many small groups decide to work together in some form of outreach. This can be a practical way of applying what you have learned. You can host a series of evangelistic discussions for your friends or neighbors. You can visit people at a home for the elderly. Help a widow with cleaning or repair jobs around her home. Such projects can have a transforming influence on your group.

For a detailed discussion of the nature and function of small groups, read *Small Group Leaders' Handbook* or *Good Things Come in Small Groups* (both from IVP).

Part 1. Liberating God's People. Exodus 1—19.
Study 1. Israel's Oppression: Evil Plans, Courageous Resistance. Exodus 1.

Purpose: To discover the depths of Israel's oppression and what is required of believers in those circumstances.

For some people, history is a big yawn. Make the study live by emphasizing the human aspects. Help the group to use their imaginations.

Question 1. Every study begins with an "approach" question, which is meant to be asked before the passage is read. These questions are important for several reasons.

First, they help the group to warm up to each other. No matter how well a group may know each other, there is always a stiffness that needs to be overcome before people will begin to talk openly. A good question will break the ice.

Second, approach questions get people thinking along the lines of the topic of the study. Most people will have lots of different things going on in their minds (dinner, an important meeting coming up, how to get the car fixed) that will have nothing to do with the study. A creative question will get their attention and draw them into the discussion.

Third, approach questions can reveal where our thoughts or feelings need to be transformed by Scripture. This is why it is especially important not to read the passage before the approach question is asked. The passage will tend to color the honest reactions people would otherwise give because they are, of course, supposed to think the way the Bible does. Giving honest responses to various issues before they find out what the Bible says may help them to see where their thoughts or attitudes need to be changed.

Question 2. Seventy people and a large number of household slaves had come to Egypt. By the time of the exodus, the Israelites numbered about 600,000 men, "besides women and children" (Ex 12:37).

Question 3. Do not skip over Joseph's crucial role in saving Egypt. Nearly three hundred years have elapsed since his death and the end of Genesis. Egypt is at the height of her power under a new dynasty of pharaohs. A great building program is begun in the fertile delta region. There is a large labor force in the area. Also, Pharaoh is uneasy about an alien group on his borders. The foreigners, called the Israelites, are shepherds of a religion that sacrificed bulls, regarded as sacred by the Egyptians. The process of making the Israelites slaves lasted many years, through the reigns of several pharaohs. In the end, the Israelites lost their land, possessions, courage (with rare exceptions), and desire to be free (2:13-14).

Question 4. Get several ideas quickly. Do not get into political debates.

Question 9. Explore in depth what it means to fear God. The root biblical idea means trust and faith in God and his Word, and hatred for anything that is contrary to his will.

Question 10. *Fear of God* is to be taken in the positive sense of accountability to him for one's actions, not in the negative sense of abject cowering before him.

Question 12. Avoid superficial generalities. Encourage people to be honest. Some may never have had the experience of finding God's help in unfair, unreasonable situations.

Study 2. The Birth and Escape of Moses: A Mother's Faith, a Son's Brashness. Exodus 2.

Purpose: To gain insight into both personal courage and brashness, pride and the consequences of failure.

Question 2. Pharaoh's daughter would probably be a daughter by one of his concubines, not a princess of royal blood. She would have taken Moses to the harem where he would be brought up learning to read and write, and gaining expertise in various skills and sports (see Acts 7:22). It was not unusual for foreigners to be brought up like this and given responsible positions in the army, civil service or priesthood. The name *Moses* means "to draw out of the water." Children often were named after important events (see v. 22).

Question 6. Midian, on the eastern gulf of the Red Sea, was inhabited by shepherds descended from Keturah, one of the wives of Abraham. They worshiped the true God and their chief, Jethro (also called Reuel), was also their priest.

Question 10. Allow time for people to think before speaking. Do not rush or force people into answering personal questions too quickly. Silent reflection is a valuable time during Bible study.

Question 13. Personal responses may come slowly, especially during the first few group discussions. It takes time for a group to establish an identity and a setting where people feel safe with each other. As trust and confidence grow, people will talk about personal ideas in more depth.

Study 3. The Call of Moses: Stubborn Reluctance Overcome. Exodus 3—4.

Purpose: To learn to trust God in the face of seemingly overwhelming obstacles.

Question 1. You may have to set a time limit on this discussion. Ask people to give concise answers, and do not permit criticism of specific leaders known to the group.

Question 2. "The mountain of God" was Mount Sinai, where God gave the Law to Israel (19:1-25). Horeb was the range of mountains that included Sinai.

"The angel of the Lord" means that God himself was present in the bush in the form of a flame of fire. As a sinful man, Moses had to be told not to draw near to God. He realized his unfitness even to look (v. 6). Taking off the shoes was a sign of respect and showed Moses' reverence for the presence of God.

Question 7. God identified himself as "I AM" (v. 14). Moses was not asking for a name-tag identification to put on God. He wants to know the significance of what God had told him in verse 6. "I AM" means that God is dependable and strong enough to meet every need of the people.

"A three-day journey" (3:18) was a way of expressing distance. A day's journey might be as much as 24 miles.

"Every woman is to ask her neighbor" (3:22). The Egyptians had oppressed the Israelites for years and made them work for very low wages. This strategy enabled them to get what was really due them, and was not dishonest.

Encourage the group to read next week's passage prior to the meeting, so that the material can be scanned during the session.

Study 4. The Difficulties of Moses and Aaron: Rebuff and Resolution. Exodus 5:1—7:7.

Purpose: To find resources in God when everything seems to be going wrong.

If group members have read this week's passage prior to the meeting, scan the material during the session, rather than reading it verse by verse. Cover the factual questions quickly so you will have ample time for discussing questions of interpretation and application.

Question 2. "Let my people go, so that they may hold a festival to me in the desert" (v. 1) is a test case. Israel had to leave Egypt to sacrifice because their sacrifices were offensive to the Egyptians (8:26). Pharaoh's refusal reveals his hostility, previously predicted by God (3:19).

"Access to Pharaoh: Rameses II is known to have made himself available even to ordinary petitioners (compare 5:11ff.). Moses, brought up in the harem, had a special claim to Pharaoh's attention" (David Alexander and Patricia Alexander, eds., *Eerdmans' Handbook to the Bible* [Grand Rapids, Mich.: Eerdmans, 1973], p. 157).

Question 8. The name *the Lord* (v. 3) was not unknown to the patriarchs, but they did not know all that the name implied. The full significance of God's character would be revealed to these helpless slaves.

A "covenant" (v. 4) is a promise and an agreement (see Gen 15:18). To "redeem" (v. 6) means "to buy back." Because the Israelites were slaves, God (as it were) bought them back their freedom. This is the pattern of Christ's redemption of sinners on the cross.

The genealogy (6:14-25) shows the lineage of Moses and Aaron. It shows the steadily unfolding plan of God. With 7:1 the story picks up and God reveals his plan for the confrontation with Pharaoh.

Question 14. Conclude your time together with prayer, thanking God for significant people and circumstances.

Study 5. The Plagues: God's Power on the Line against Pharaoh. Exodus 7:8—10:29.

Purpose: To recognize the futility of trying to withstand God.

This is a long section to study. Emphasize the skill of reading for major trends. There is not time to discuss many interesting details.

Question 2. Humanistic explanations of the plagues on Egypt abound. For those who want to explore answers from scholars who accept the biblical text at face value, point out various reference works such as the *New Bible Dictionary, 2d ed.,* J. D. Douglas, ed. (Wheaton, Ill.: Tyndale, 1982).

The Nile River was the heart of Egypt's economy and worship. The Egyptian magicians counterfeited some of the plagues, but they were powerless to stop God's judgment. Two of the magicians are named in 2 Timothy 3:8. They used Satanic powers to oppose God.

The first three plagues were over all the land, and they affected both Israelites and Egyptians. The next six were on the Egyptians only and not over the land of Goshen where the Israelites lived.

Question 3. Several times in this story God is said to have hardened Pharaoh's heart (4:21; 10:1, 20, 27). This was not done against Pharaoh's will. God could have softened Pharaoh's heart, but he simply let him be. In New Testament terms, God gave him over—let him be what he himself wanted to be;

let him have his own way—so that in the end God's power would be plain for all to see (see Rom 1:18-32; 9:17).

Question 8. The point is not to conclude that all natural disasters are God's judgment, but to explore reasons why many people prefer to talk about "bad luck," as if there were no personal God controlling the universe he made.

Question 10. Pharaoh wanted to keep his hold on the Israelites by giving them part of what they asked. He suggested four compromises (8:25, 28; 10:11, 24) to keep them in or near Egypt. God's enemy, Satan, uses the same strategy with God's children today, suggesting compromises rather than full obedience, to prevent them from enjoying the fullness of God's blessing.

Question 11. Do not accept glib answers. Take time for the group to probe for a number of serious responses.

End with the redemptive emphasis of the study's final question, so people will be aware of the needs of others.

Study 6. The Passover: Night of Death and Deliverance. Exodus 11:1 —12:28.

Purpose: To appreciate and praise God for delivering Israel and for giving us Christ, our Passover lamb.

Because of the crucial tie-in between the Old and New Testaments regarding the Passover, this story requires careful study. It also requires a confrontation with Jesus Christ. For some, this may be their first realization of what Jesus did for them on the cross.

The story takes a decisive turn at the end of chapter 11. The acts of God in which there is no redemption are over. They are distinct from God's redemption to come. The Passover sacrifice protected the Israelites and gave them the deliverance that the earlier plagues could not secure.

Question 6. Refer again to the note in Study 5, Question 3, about the hardening of Pharaoh's heart.

Question 9. "This applies only to this celebration, but the point is of permanent relevance; the redeemed are committed to pilgrimage" (D. Guthrie & J. A. Motyer, eds., *The New Bible Commentary, Revised* [Grand Rapids, Mich.: Eerdmans, 1970], p. 127).

Question 10. "Unleavened bread" is bread made without yeast.

Question 14. Be sure to allow time for studying the New Testament references. Give people a chance to reflect quietly. Don't push them into saying things.

Study 7. The Exodus: Freedom and Its Cost. Exodus 12:29—13:16.
Purpose: To grasp the implications of God's gift of spiritual freedom.
Question 2. For earlier encounters see, for example, 8:25-32; 9:27-35; 10:10-11, 16-20, 27-29; 11:10.
"Six hundred thousand men on foot" (v. 37) means those who could bear arms. On the basis of general population statistics, this figure would imply a total of more than two million Israelites—men, women and children. "Many other people" (v. 38) refers to Egyptians who had married Israelites, plus other Semites who had migrated to Egypt. "Four hundred and thirty years" (vv. 40-41) begins with the entry of Jacob into Egypt (46:6-7).
Question 4. Take time to trace the earlier passages, so you get an overall understanding of the revelation of God. Your knowledge depends on the accumulation of evidence.
Question 5. Look for specific comments, not vague generalizations.
Question 8. Perhaps you will have to summarize for some what are the distinctive, essential elements of the Christian faith: the deity of Christ, salvation only through faith in his name, and the necessity of repentance and faith for salvation.
Question 9. "Consecrate to me" (v. 1) means to set apart for God, as, for example, a soldier is recruited for duty. Because God had delivered the firstborn from judgment, he had a claim on them. In the New Testament the same basic logic is applied to Christians, who are set apart to be holy to God because they have been saved from the judgment of their sin by the death and resurrection of Christ (see Heb 10:10-14).
"Sign on your hand and a reminder on your forehead" (vv. 9, 16) are metaphorical references to the Egyptian custom of wearing amulets containing written words. Later, the Jews had a similar practice while at prayer. Phylacteries bound on the head and the left hand contained handwritten copies of Exodus 13:1-16 (see Deut 6:4-9; 11:13-21).
The donkey (v. 13), a representative of unclean animals, was valuable as a beast of burden. It was to be redeemed or destroyed.
Question 11. Allow time for thoughtful reflection and practical answers.

Study 8. Crossing the Red Sea: From Crisis to Triumph. Exodus 13:17—14:31.
Purpose: To learn to trust God in the midst of crisis.
This story probably has more obvious application to events in your life than any of Israel's experiences thus far. You may have to keep the group moving through the questions (for example, question 8) to be sure you cover them

all. Avoid the temptation to gloss over or to generalize questions that call for personal answers.

Question 2. The most direct route from Egypt to Palestine was the coastal road from Rameses to Gaza, along the Mediterranean shore. Consult a Bible lands map.

Question 4. See Genesis 50:24-25 for the reference to Joseph (v. 19).

Question 6. "No graves in Egypt" reveals sarcasm, because Egypt was famous for its graves, the pyramids, which were tombs.

Question 11. The crossing was miraculous in the sense that God used a natural agent (a strong east wind) with supernatural results (dividing the waters).

Question 14. Encourage a time of praise for past mercies and specific evidences of God's power and love.

Study 9. The Songs of Moses and Miriam: Praise for the Past and Hope for the Future. Exodus 15:1-21.

Purpose: To develop new skills in worship as an outgrowth of our relationship with God.

The subject of this study will be unfamiliar to most people. We rarely discuss the essence of worship. Therefore, group responses may be slow. The leader should not answer the questions, but rather be a gentle encourager and persistent guide.

Question 4. This may take some time to answer. Encourage the group to give practical, not theoretical, answers.

Question 8. Probably a new application for some who are not used to thinking of God in this way. Have some of your own ideas prepared to keep the discussion on track.

Question 12. Think about an illustration of this principle on the personal level. What elements go into building security?

Question 15. Avoid debates about personal likes and dislikes in worship services. Summarize the reasons why Israel's experience of worship on this occasion was so meaningful.

Study 10. Adversities of the Desert: Thirst, Hunger and Attack—God Overcomes Them All. Exodus 15:22—17:16.

Purpose: To discover reactions prompted by adversity and how they deter our obedience to God.

Question 2. After reading these verses, turn to a map in the back of the Bible to locate the desert where these events took place. Briefly summarize what the Sinai Peninsula is like.

Marah was reached after a journey of 30 to 40 miles.

Question 4. Insist on complete candor here. No dodging the issue with cliches.

Question 7. "The common quail migrated across the Red Sea in large numbers at this time and, faint after a long journey, could be caught with ease. The miraculous element consists in the time of their arrival" (*The New Bible Commentary, Revised,* p. 129).

Manna (16:15, 31) comes from the Hebrew word meaning "What is it?" Several things like it are known to exist in Sinai, but nothing matches it exactly. Manna remains wholly in the realm of the supernatural. This substance was Israel's staple food for forty years, ceasing abruptly when they entered Canaan.

Question 8. An "omer" (vv. 16, 18) was a small measuring bowl of about four pints.

Question 9. Come prepared with some ideas of your own. This is probably a new subject for some.

Question 11. The Amalekites were a branch of the Edomite race, descendants of Esau (Gen 36:12, 16). They were a nomadic people especially hostile to Israel (see Deut 25:17-18).

Question 12. Many avenues are available, but generally Christians are too introspective to think about using them. Most of the applications in this study are personal. Here is a chance to think about the needs of society.

Study 11. Jethro's Counsel: Enlist Helpers to Carry the Load. Exodus 18.

Purpose: To find God's way for exercising leadership.

This chapter touches on a little-known episode. It raises questions and issues rarely discussed. The action is relatively simple, but the implications are profound. Do not avoid them in discussion just because everyone is not an official leader.

Question 2. It is not clear when Zipporah had gone back to her father's home. Perhaps it was soon after the incident recorded in 4:24-26.

Question 5. Jethro worships God by bringing a burnt offering and other sacrifices. Sacrifice was practiced before the giving of the Law to Israel at Mount Sinai.

Question 6. Family worship is not the prime thrust of this story, but it is an important matter in Christian living. It is worth raising in this context, but limit discussion.

Question 8. The new arrangement was not forced on Moses. It was first submitted to him for his consideration, and then he was to seek God's will in the matter (v. 23).

Question 11. After thinking about your openness to God's counsel, talk about how this counsel sometimes happens. Give a personal example.

Question 13. Some may find it hard to accept the role of ego-building in serving God. They are a minority, but it is helpful to raise the issue.

Study 12. The Encampment at Mount Sinai: Preparation for God's Laws. Exodus 19.

Purpose: To consider refreshing ways to hear God's voice.

Question 2. We stand on the threshold of a new stage in God's relationship with Israel. He was their King and they were his people, chosen to keep his law, live for him, and be a witness to his truth before the surrounding nations. Their encampment at Mt. Sinai was the fulfillment of God's promise (see 3:12). The Israelites stayed there for nearly a year. The "Desert of Sinai" would be the open land before the mountain. "A holy nation" (19:5) is one separated from other nations and devoted to God.

Question 4. Seek specific answers that people can relate to, not vague, pious generalities.

Question 5. The abstinence from sexual intercourse stands in sharp contrast to other ancient religions in which sensuous orgies were incorporated into the rituals. God did not give this requirement because sex was considered sinful, but because the people might have become ceremonially unclean (Lev 15:18-19).

Question 13. This is the key point in personal application. Gauge discussion time, and encourage personal reflection before verbalizing.

Question 14. Take time for careful reading of this passage. Know what facts you want the group to find.

Part 2. Teaching God's People. Exodus 20—40.

Study 1. The Ten Commandments: Keys to God's Character and Human Welfare. Exodus 20:1-21.

Purpose: To learn how and why God's moral laws are best for humanity.

Each of the Ten Commandments warrants a full-length study. You will have to be judicious in the use of time and in sensing which commands the group seems most interested in exploring.

Question 2. There were three stages in the giving of the Law. First, God spoke to Moses, who told the people (Ex 20—24); second, Moses went up

Mount Sinai for forty days and received the two tablets of stone and the instructions for the tabernacle and priests (Ex 25—32); third, Moses made the second tablets of stone after he had broken the first tablets because the people sinned, and God again wrote on them (Ex 34).

The Law itself included three parts: (1) The Ten Commandments (20:1-26); (2) the judgments (21:1—24:11); (3) the ordinances (24:12—31:18). The first four commands concern our relationship to God, the remaining six our relationship to one another. Hence Jesus' two-clause summary of the Law in Matthew 22:37-40.

Question 3. *Before me* (v. 3) has connotations of one who would be God's rival. No one or no thing is to take God's supreme place in our lives.

Question 4. God is a "jealous" God (v. 5) in the sense that he "will not allow what is his just due in terms of reverence and obedience to be given to anything else" *(The New Bible Commentary, Revised,* p. 132). This is part of his innately righteous character.

"Punishing the children for the sin of the fathers" (v. 5) indicates certain ongoing social and physical consequences of sin. Those thus punished are those who "hate" God. At the same time, God's mercy to those who love and obey him reaches a thousand generations.

Question 7. The point is to keep one day in seven. Some churches observe Saturday, but most Sunday, because of New Testament worship on the day of Christ's resurrection. In some Muslim countries Christians worship on Friday.

Question 12. Counselors agree that robbery victims, for example, or even those whose homes have been burglarized, feel much more than the loss of possessions. They feel that they themselves, their inner spirits, have been wounded. They have been harmed personally.

Question 13. This prohibits lying, particularly in a court of law, as well as defamation of character.

Study 2. Laws for Israel: God's Concern for a Well-Ordered Society. Exodus 20:22—23:19.

Purpose: To look at the big moral and social issues that confront society.

The group will have to make a huge historical and cultural jump to apply this text. It is too easy to dismiss it as irrelevant. We must take time to discover the principles of holiness as they apply to Israel before we attempt to discuss their contemporary relevance. In the Bible, moral and religious laws are inseparable, showing God's concern for all of life. There is one law for all, whatever a person's status. A high view of human life is demonstrated by fixed, limited penalties.

Question 2. The "altar of earth or uncut stone" (v. 25) signified the simplicity of true worship and the access to God given to every Israelite. Going up steps would cause immodest exposure of nakedness.

Question 3. A person could be born a slave, be sold into slavery by his parents, be sold for theft or insolvency, or he might be obliged to sell himself.

Question 4. For unpremeditated homicide the penalty was modified, and cities of refuge were appointed later (see Deut 19:1-13).

Question 8. Sorcerers (v. 18) were utterly opposed to the whole religion and faith of Israel, and were to be destroyed. A sorceress (or witch) was one who foretold the future by the power of Satan.

The poor were not to be at the mercy of the rich (v. 25). No essential article was to be kept as collateral, such as a cloak (v. 26), which served as a coat by day and a blanket by night. The moneylender was not to charge excessive interest, or usury.

Question 13. These brief instructions (vv. 10-13) were for Israel to observe in the wilderness. Later, in Leviticus, fuller instructions are given for how the feasts were to be observed when they reached Canaan (Lev 23—25). The seventh year (v. 10) and the seventh day were to be honored for both philanthropic and economic reasons. Verse 18 refers to the Passover. The fat is the choice part of the sacrifice which was to be burned. "Do not cook a young goat in its mother's milk" (v. 19) refers to a pagan practice of trying to increase fertility and productivity by magical arts.

Study 3. Ratifying the Covenant: God's Call to His People Confirmed. Exodus 23:20—24:18.
Purpose: To sense our duty to be faithful to commitments made to God.

This study requires careful consideration of contemporary parallels. Basic principles of God-human relationships undergird the ceremonies. Take time to think through relevant New Testament ideas and their application.

Question 2. The "sacred stones" (v. 24) were idolatrous stones carved with symbols of pagan worship. The "hornet" (v. 28) is a metaphorical description of God's activity.

Question 3. The "Sea of the Philistines" (v. 31) is the Mediterranean; "from the desert to the River" meant from the desert south of Palestine to the River Euphrates in the northeast. Consult a Bible lands map.

Question 6. Nadab and Abihu (v. 1) were two of Aaron's sons who later died after committing sacrilege (Lev 10:1-2).

The significance of blood is that of atoning death. Reflect again on the Passover. The blood was first sprinkled on the altar (v. 6) to show the demand to satisfy God's wrath against sin. After the people promised to obey God, they were sprinkled with blood (v. 8). "It is in the context of their attempt to walk the way of holiness that God's people become aware of the need of atoning blood (see 1 Jn 1:7—2:2)" *(The New Bible Commentary, Revised,* p. 134).

Question 10. Having a meal with someone (v. 11) is the essence of fellowship in the Near East. In verses 9-11 the writer gropes for words to describe the indescribable communion that followed the sacrifice and fulfilled the covenant.

Question 11. "Forty days and forty nights" (v. 18) shows that certain numbers have special significance in the Bible. The round number forty occurs at almost every new stage in Israel's history: the flood, the time of the spies in Canaan, Elijah's journey to Horeb, Jesus' time in the wilderness, and the time between his resurrection and ascension.

Study 4. Instructions for the Tabernacle: God's Blueprint for Worship. Exodus 25—27.

Purpose: To appreciate anew God's provision for meaningful worship.

Reading these chapters may put you to sleep. Here's where a Bible dictionary will help. Study the sketches. Don't worry about getting all the details. Emphasize big principles and important applications for worship today.

Question 2. Acacia wood (v. 5) came from the abundant acacia trees on Sinai. They are about as tall as mulberry trees, and their wood is very hard. The "ephod" (v. 7) was part of the clothing of the high priest. The word *tabernacle* (v. 9) means a dwelling place. It was a very beautiful tent in which the Israelites could worship God as they journeyed from place to place. God gave very careful instructions for its construction.

Question 3. Assign these texts to different people to read aloud.

Question 4. Don't take too much time debating the second question.

Question 5. This ark was unique in that it housed the Law, not an image. It was the center of Israel's divinely revealed religion. "Everything pointed to it. Three matching entrances (26:31-32, 36-37; 27:16-17) led to it—for the purpose of entering the court of the tabernacle was to enter the presence of God himself. Along the path leading to the ark lay the altar of burnt-offering (27:1-8), the altar of incense (30:1-6), and the mercy seat where the blood of sacrifice was finally sprinkled (25:17ff.; Lev 16:14)—showing that it was only by sacrifice, prayer and the effectiveness of shed blood that man could come to God" *(Eerdmans' Handbook to the Bible,* p. 168).

The "cubit" (v. 10) was about a foot and a half.

"The Testimony" (v. 16) was the tablets of stone which God later gave to

Moses with the Law written on them. The "atonement cover" (v. 17) was a rectangular plate on top of the ark. The Hebrew word for this means "to cover," but in the form it is used here it means "to make atonement." It was not merely a covering lid, but a sacred object in itself. The "cherubim" (v. 18) were two gold figures representing angels.

Question 6. See 16:33 for the origin of the bread of the Presence (v. 30). It consisted of twelve baked cakes set out in two rows. Frankincense was placed on each row, and they were offered to the Lord by fire.

The lampstand (vv. 31-40) was the only source of light in the sanctuary. All natural light was shut out by design. New Testament scholars see the lamp as an illustration of Jesus as the light of the world (see Jn 8:12).

Question 8. The "curtain" (v. 31) hung between the holy place and the most holy place where the ark was. Its meaning is fully explained in Hebrews 10:20. When Jesus was crucified, the curtain in the temple was torn in two from top to bottom, symbolizing that the way to God had been opened to all through Jesus.

Questions 10-11. "The whole structure of the tabernacle speaks clear and splendid truths. It provides a visible summary of the central affirmations of the Bible: that God indwells his people (see 1 Cor 3:16; Eph 2:19-22); that he intends his people to worship him according to his will and not their own whim (Mark 7:6-13); and that only by means of sacrifice and shed blood can sinners ever come to live with the Holy One (Eph 2:11-18; Heb 10:19-25)" (*Eerdmans' Handbook to the Bible,* p. 168).

Study 5. Instituting the Priesthood: God's Holiness Demonstrated. Exodus 28:1—29:37.
Purpose: To consider Israel's priesthood and to appreciate its fulfillment in the person of Christ.

This study requires a grasp of two long sections of material from Exodus, plus the important New Testament teaching about Jesus our high priest from Hebrews. Not every fact is discussed. Keep the study moving. Plan adequate time for the last two questions.

Question 2. "Sacred garments" (v. 2) does not mean that the actual clothes were holy, but that they were put to holy use. The Hebrew word for *sacred* in this verse is the same word translated "consecrate" in 13:2 and "consecration" in 28:3.

The high priest wore (1) the "tunic" (28:39), a robe of fine linen worn next to the skin; (2) the "sash" (vv. 4, 39), a long seamless garment trimmed around the hem with tassels in the form of pomegranates, and little bells; (3)

the "ephod" (vv. 6-12), a short linen coat reaching from the shoulder to the knee and embroidered in gold, purple and scarlet; (4) the "breastpiece" (vv. 15-19), a pouch of linen to which was attached a gold framework containing twelve jewels engraved with the names of the twelve tribes; (6) the "turban" (vv. 36-38) adorned with a gold-engraved band.

"Urim and Thummim" (v. 30) means "curses and perfections." Some scholars think they were two special stones used in drawing lots when seeking God's will on national problems. (See Lev 8:8; Num 27:21; Deut 33:8; 1 Sam 28:6; Ezra 2:63; Neh 7:65.)

Question 8. "Everything about this elaborate ceremonial points to the 'otherness' of God's people. He will be with his people, but there can be no familiarity. He is to be approached only in the ways he lays down. Sin disqualifies all men from entering God's presence. The priests and every item of equipment must be specially set apart for service. So Aaron and his sons must be cleansed, robed and their sins expiated by sacrifice before they may take office. The living God is no impotent image to be worshiped as a man thinks fit. He lays down the only terms on which it is possible for him to take up residence with his people" *(Eerdmans' Handbook to the Bible,* p. 169).

Study 6. Planning the Tabernacle: God's Revelation in People and Things. Exodus 29:38—31:18.

Purpose: To get excited about worship and the potential of using our gifts for God.

It is difficult to make worship a practical, relevant subject. Usually we think very little about it. Look for the significance of the major parts of God's plan, as well as the various New Testament parallels. Allow time for the important summary question 14. Do not take time to discuss every detail of these chapters.

Question 2. Everything is made holy, not by the intrinsic worth of the things used, but by the spiritual presence of God visibly displayed.

Question 6. This was not a tax. The money provided not only for the worship within the tabernacle, but also as a reminder that the people were preserved by God's mercy. The amount was small, so everyone could afford it, and because it demonstrated that no amount could redeem them.

Question 10. The anointing oil signified the bestowal of the Holy Spirit for special purposes. It was not to be used for general purposes. In fact, everything related to the worship of God was consecrated by it. If properly used, it would be a means of grace and blessing to the worshipers. Note the severe warnings in verses 33 and 38.

Study 7. The Golden Calf: Idolatry Takes a Fearful Toll. Exodus 32.
Purpose: To see the consequences of disobedience and to learn how we can stay faithful to God.
Question 2. Moses was up in the mountain for forty days (24:18). This is what happened in the camp while he was absent.
Question 3. The calf image shows the continued influence of Egyptian idolatry. Animals were sacred, and gods were represented with animals' heads and bodies. One of the cults was the cult of the bull, Apis. "Revelry" (v. 6) was an orgiastic dance that characterized pagan religions.
Question 4. The basis of Moses' intercession and the ground of his hope is God's honor. God's relenting (v. 14) is a change in his dealings with his people, not a change in his character or purposes.
Question 10. When restraints are removed, not only do the people suffer, but God's honor is corrupted, and consequently the people must be purged.
Question 12. "Blot me out of the book you have written" (v. 32) is an expression taken from the practice of keeping registers of citizens.

Study 8. God's Presence and Glory: Essential Requirement and Goal. Exodus 33.
Purpose: To understand why God's presence means total sufficiency for all our needs.
Question 5. These verses show how worship was carried out before the tabernacle was completed. The tabernacle later came to be called the tent of meeting. "Face to face" (v. 11) is to be taken metaphorically, as the following words show. God and Moses had unrestricted communion; nothing was withheld, nothing hidden.
Question 8. God's presence bestows favor and assurance on his people and marks them out as his own, for his glory. Therefore, Moses concludes his appeal on the basis of God's covenant with Israel.
Question 9. In verse 17 the Lord tells Moses that he knows him by name. In verse 19 the Lord reciprocates by allowing Moses to hear his name proclaimed. Thus their relationship becomes more two-sided and personal.
Question 12. "You cannot see my face" (v. 20) is not a contradiction of Moses' experience in 24:10. No one has ever seen God the Father (Deut 4:15; Jn 1:18), but only some outward sign of his presence, something like a bright cloud or a great blaze of light, whose brilliance could only be described as being like sapphires.
Question 13. Be sure the ideas are practical, not theoretical. Allow time for quiet reflection before asking people to verbalize their thoughts.

Study 9. Renewing the Covenant: God Reveals His Nature and Laws— Again. Exodus 34.
Purpose: To gain new appreciation of God's forgiveness and motivation to serve him fully.
Question 2. There is no contradiction between verse 1 and verses 27-28. In verse 27 Moses is commanded to write the contents of the preceding verses— "these words"; in verse 28 God is the subject of the last verb and not Moses. This chapter is an abridged form of the "book of the covenant," with promises and warnings justified by Israel's recent failure and the forthcoming temptations of Canaan.
Question 3. Martin Luther called verses 6-7 "the sermon on the Name." God's love, mercy and forgiveness are set alongside his justice, righteousness and judgment of sin.
Question 6. "Sacred stones" and "Asherah poles" (v. 13) were stone and wooden idols devoted to pagan deities.
Question 8. "Those in covenant with the one living God cannot align themselves with pagan beliefs or religious practices; they must exterminate them. The people of God must be pure" (*The New Bible Commentary, Revised,* p. 138).
Question 9. Have these verses read aloud by different people. Take sufficient time to dig out the relevant principles.
Questions 13-14. Allow ample time for personal reflection. Seek simple, practical responses.

Study 10. Building the Tabernacle: More Than Enough to Do the Job. Exodus 35—36.
Purpose: To be excited by Israel's generosity and to learn how to give the same way.
These chapters may at first glance appear to be repetitious, but look for the exciting way in which Israel responded to the challenge to build. Unfortunately, some appeals for money are not biblically based. This episode offers a chance to look at giving in a fresh way.
Question 4. Think of such things as pride, dignity and self-respect that come from ownership and not from accepting handouts.
Question 9. Some illustrations of the tabernacle from a Bible dictionary will help here.
Question 10. Many people suffer from low self-image. Encourage everyone to take time to think about what they enjoy doing and about what others encourage them in doing. God's gifts to us are intended for the enrichment

of others (see 1 Pet 4:10-11).
Question 12. Avoid being judgmental. Talk over the basic spiritual require-
ments in each person's life.

**Study 11. Making Furnishings and Garments: God Speaks Powerfully
in Wood, Gold, Silver, Linen and Wool. Exodus 37:1—39:31.**
Purpose: To learn about God and ourselves through the tabernacle's furnishings and the priests' garments.
  This is a long section to read and study. It repeats the instructions given
to Moses earlier. Take time to probe the major significance of the facts, as well
as the New Testament passages. There will not be time to delve into all the
details of the furniture.
Question 2. Refresh your understanding of the tabernacle's furnishings by
checking a Bible dictionary.
Question 4. Those who have been Christians for some time will need to
encourage younger believers in thinking through their responses.
Question 6. Refer to the Leader's Notes in Study 5.
Question 7. This may be a new thought to some. Make clear that the priesthood Peter talks about is not related to any official church role or position.
Questions 8-9. Allow ample time for these questions. Ask people to be
specific in their answers.
Question 10. This question gives an opportunity to show the consistency of
scriptural truth and how certain ideas are reinforced because of it. It helps
us appreciate God's hand in the inspiration of the Bible.

**Study 12. Dedicating the Tabernacle: Time for Praise and Reflection.
Exodus 39:32—40:38.**
Purpose: To join in the praise of God with thoughtful thanksgiving for his
goodness.
Question 3. Be sensitive to the comments made. This is an agonizing issue
for many people because they are unsure they have found or followed God's
will.
Question 4. God gave the instructions about how and in what order the
tabernacle was to be set up. The emphasis is on the consecration, washing
and investiture of the priests.
Question 7. The cloud was the visible evidence of God's favor. God makes
clear that the tabernacle, the center of Israel's life, is the divinely ordained
place of worship.
Question 11. For three hundred years, until it was replaced by the temple

in Solomon's day, the tabernacle remained the focal point of the nation's worship.

Question 12. Plan enough time here. It is important to solidify gains made throughout the entire study. To do that, people need to speak up. They will remember what they said more than what someone else tells them.

James Reapsome is executive director of Evangelical Missions Information Service and the author of Romans: A Daily Dialogue with God *(Harold Shaw). He is coauthor with his wife, Martha, of* Marriage: God's Design for Intimacy *(IVP).*